Welcome to Your Life

Bahareh Amidi

Copyright © 2024 Bahareh Amidi. All Rights Reserved.
ISBN 978-0-578-78713-8

cover and interior illustrations by
   Roberta Sarada Enzmann:
   www.roberta-illustration.com

email: connect@bahareh.com
facebook.com/Bahareh.Amidi
twitter.com/BaharehAmidi
youtube.com/baharehLIVE
instagram.com/bahareh_poetess
www.bahareh.com

"There was once a road through the woods…"

RUDY KIPLING
The Way Through The Woods

Listen to Welcome to Your Life

There was once a way through my thoughts
There was once a breath easy to take
There was once a smile always on my face
   —in my heart

In all that I try to recall
I tend to forget
The simmering truths that always remain
The truths that only my heart can see on days
    I wake before dawn

There is perhaps not one road through the woods
But indeed each and every branch point the way
   to the roads that lead the way to Thee
The maps set forth by the roots of the trees
The tenderness of such beauty of the day of resurrection
Every fallen leaf on my path becomes a mirror
   and therein I see the truth of Thy making

The dawn holds the truths
the days come and go
Revelations revealed on roads less traveled
Those roads going through the forest
Those roads going through the sea ready to part
The parting of the seas
a symbol of possibilities only
    and only if I am ready to receive
My hands cupped together asking you to pour your light
    —regardless of forest or sea

I am learning to swim in the forest
I am learning to walk through the seas
I only tend to lose my way
    when I seek guidance from other than Thee
I am here completely blank—
emotions reveal
   colors show
      letters speak

And yet I remain not deaf and dumb not mute,
    not a puppet nor a puppeteer
I remain aware of my Breath and knowing you will lead the way
I will take off my mask
I will take off my shoes
With my bare soul
    I seek to be moved into thy Light
Through the mist
    I arrive
        I smile
Hello Bahareh welcome to your life

www.ingramcontent.com/pod-product-compliance
Lightning Source LLC
Chambersburg PA
CBHW061803290426
44109CB00030B/2927